MW00893289

Potty Training for Beginners

A Comprehensive Step-by-step Guide to an Easy Potty Transition for Toddlers

Book 2 of the Mindful Child Series

Freya Gates

Legal & Disclaimer

The information contained in this book and its contents is not designed to replace or take the place of any form of medical or professional advice; and is not meant to replace the need for independent medical, financial, legal or other professional advice or services, as may be required. The content and information in this book has been provided for educational and entertainment purposes only.

The content and information contained in this book has been compiled from sources deemed reliable, and it is accurate to the best of the Author's knowledge, information and belief. However, the Author cannot guarantee its accuracy and validity and cannot be held liable for any errors and/or omissions. Further, changes are periodically made to this book as and when needed. Where appropriate and/or necessary, you must consult a professional (including but not limited to your doctor, attorney, financial advisor or such other professional advisor) before using any of the suggested remedies, techniques, or information in this book.

Upon using the contents and information contained in this book, you agree to hold harmless the Author from and against any damages, costs, and expenses, including any legal fees potentially resulting from the application of any of the information provided by this book. This disclaimer applies to any loss, damages or injury caused by the use and application, whether directly or indirectly, of any advice or information presented, whether for breach of contract, tort, negligence, personal injury, criminal intent, or under any other cause of action.

You agree to accept all risks of using the information presented inside this book.

You agree that by continuing to read this book, where appropriate and/or necessary, you shall consult a professional (including but not limited to your doctor, attorney, or financial advisor or such other advisor as needed) before using any of the suggested remedies, techniques, or information in this book.

Contents

Introduction

Potty training your child or toddler can be an intimidating situation, but it shouldn't be that way. It's natural to second-guess yourself and all the efforts you put into helping out your child. The good thing is that you are definitely not alone in this. While there is a myriad of tips out there to guide you, potty training isn't a one-size-fits-all kind of thing. It all boils down to the unique little individual that you are trying to potty train.

The goal of this book is to make this phase as smooth as possible for you and your child. This book has a little something for everyone – whether you are a first-timer, potty trained in the past and hit a few snags, or if you're a true-blue veteran in this department.

The best way to approach potty training is to see it as an adventure. Yep, that's right. This messy, confusing, and chaotic duty is a beautiful transition, rather than an inconvenience. As an adult, you will be the source of help and comfort. No matter how difficult it is for you to train them, just imagine how confusing and overwhelming it is for them. Freedom and independence are huge milestones, and all developmental milestones need your loving support.

Imagine learning to dance the tango with no prior experience. You would need the right stuff, the right clothes, the right shoes, and of course, the most supportive dance teacher to help you out. In potty training, the excitement of buying the right gear should be an exciting time for your toddler. The pleasure of owning new things will allow them to set aside the fear and anxiety they harbour. Likewise, you as the teacher should be mentally prepared. Only then can you and your child reach your potty-training goals.

Chapter 1: Is Your Child Ready?

This is perhaps the most hotly debated part of potty training. Over-anxious parents who don't want to deal with the bother of diapers anymore often try to force their child into using the toilet before they are ready.

This can be highly detrimental to them, however, and you must wait until your child shows signs of readiness before you begin. If you don't, this will be a very long process filled with frustration and headaches for both you and your child.

There is no magic age when potty training should begin. In general, most kids are ready around the age of two or two and a half and girls tend to train before boys do. Boys are often able to gain control of urine but have problems with bowel control.

Here are some common signs that your child might be ready to use the potty.

✓ Bowel movements occur at about the same time every day.

✓ He or she can stay dry for a few hours at a time or wakes up from sleep dry.

✓ Your child begins to talk about using the potty and knows when they have to go to the bathroom.

✓ They are able to tell you when they have a soiled diaper.

✓ They can understand the association between dry pants and using the potty.

✓ He or she understands the terminology such as "poop," "pee," "dry," "wet," "potty," etc.

Independence is also an important aspect of being ready for the potty. If your child can understand simple commands like "Let's go to the potty," then readiness is also imminent. There are other things to watch for as well.

✓ Your child can pull his/her pants up and down.

✓ They begin to imitate other members of the family.

✓ He or she watches you on the toilet and asks questions.

✓ Your child wants to do things by herself/himself.

✓ He or she enjoys washing his/her hands.

✓ They get upset if their belongings are not in their proper place.

✓ Your child wants to please you.

Toddlers are classically fussy little people. At a certain point in their upbringing, they will refuse to do absolutely anything for you when asked. When they have progressed beyond this stage sufficiently enough to obey simple commands, potty training can commence.

Now, don't think that this whole process is completely in your child's hands. There are some steps you can take before the actual potty process begins to prepare your child for potty training.

Helping Them Get Ready

There is much to be said for setting the stage well before you begin toilet training. Few children train themselves. They need to know what's expected of them! They need and deserve your help and guidance.

A child who has become familiar with bathroom procedures and equipment is more likely to become trained quickly and easily than one who has not. How can you best do this?

First, take your child into the bathroom with you. It's especially helpful if fathers and brothers set the example for boys, and mothers and sisters set the example for girls. Brothers or sisters are often pleased to act as role models.

Of course, there are always other children who would like to show off their potty skills to your child. If your child is in day care, they can watch how their peers use the potty and will most likely imitate them. In fact, this can actually speed up the process significantly.

Try to help your child recognize the sensations of "being wet," "wetting now," and "about to be wet." Encourage your child to talk about these sensations -- especially "about to be..." sensations without pressing your child to be toilet trained.

Comment on signs you notice, such as the child's pausing in play or walking as if he or she is uncomfortable. Use statements such as, "You are going poop," rather than asking the general question, "What are you doing?" Asking your child to let you know when the diaper is wet or messy is another way of increasing awareness.

Finding Your Child's Throne

Some people think that having a separate "facility" for your child to go in will only confuse him or her. Sometimes the whole potty training process involves introducing a potty chair and mastering that, then moving on to an adapter seat that fits over the regular toilet progressing to actually using the big toilet all the time.

This, however, isn't written in stone, and many people go about this process in different ways. Having a potty chair readily available is a great tool when teaching your child about toilet habits. It's something that is all theirs and no one else's which gives them ownership in their young life.

Believe it or not, there are all sorts of different options when choosing a potty chair and getting the right one can make all the difference in success during potty training.

Proponents of the potty chair say it allows a child to be more independent, since a parent doesn't need to lift the child to the toilet.

It also allows a child to place his or her feet squarely on the floor when bearing down while pooping, and the child can also use the support of the chair's arms.

As we've said, because a potty chair is obviously the child's own, he or she will take pride in possessing it. Choosing the right potty chair should begin as soon as your child shows an interest in using the potty. Involve him or her in the process of picking out their own chair.

If you have a potty in the bathroom, you and your child can go to the toilet at the same time. For some adults, this is a frightening thought as their privacy means the world to them, but it can make all the difference during the training process.

One disadvantage is that a boy will not be able to pee standing up - it will be too difficult, and there will be too much splashing.

Another consideration is that it needs to be cleaned out by you or the child. In the beginning, cleaning out the pot will be fun. With experience, it loses its appeal for a child -- and probably for you, too.

13

If the thought of using a potty chair appeals to you, you should get one before you start training, so it becomes a familiar piece of equipment for your child. In fact, you may even let your child shop for the chair with you. You can narrow the choice down to two or three styles, and let your child choose from among those. This can make the child all the more anxious to try it.

Personalizing a potty chair will also make it more unique and interesting. You can do this by adding a few stickers or decal of your child's choosing. Or, you could also use press-type letters and spell out your child's name.

Let your child know that it's okay -- for now -- to sit on the potty with clothes on to get used to it, but when he or she is ready, it will be used like "Mommy and Daddy use the toilet." Avoid using the seat at other times so as not to confuse the issue.

Chapter 2: Myths and Misconceptions

It's time to prepare your child for the big milestone. Start by deconstructing the following misconceptions below.

Myth 1: Wait until your child gives you signals that he's ready.

This is false. To wait for signals is inviting all sorts of trouble. Your child has always peed into the diaper. He doesn't know that there is a world of toilets out there. What signal could they give when they don't know what to be signalling about?

The signals only come when potty training has begun. This can be in the form of a "pee-pee dance" such as hopping from one foot to the other. This is an effort to hold the pee. It could also be twitching or becoming angsty, or as simple as stating their need to use the potty.

Myth 2: Girls are easier to train than boys.

Girls mature faster than boys and that's why the common consensus is that they are easier to train. However, this is not true. It is more dependent on how fast a toddler learns as an individual. This is like learning to walk. A toddler could learn to walk as early as 9 months or when he reaches 15 months. Each child is case dependent.

Myth 3: Train them to pee first, only then can you train them to poop.

This is false. Kids wouldn't know if the diaper he has on is for pooping or for peeing. The only difference between the two acts would be the sensations they feel.

One of the things that does work is to let your child see how peeing and pooping is normal. Doing the act doesn't have to be a well-kept secret. It may sound unconventional but bringing your child with you to the toilet can be a good thing. While you do your stuff, have them sit, and read to them. Over time, your kid will realize that sitting on the toilet seat is a normal routine and isn't daunting.

Myth 4: Put the potty chair out before you begin training so that they will get used to it.

This is false. Putting out a potty chair for the child to get familiar with is counterproductive. The kid will start to get it confused with his toys if it is in plain sight. If he is so used to seeing it daily, he may not put any thought into the seriousness of its function. Keep things simple and only introduce the potty when it is time to begin potty training.

Chapter 3: The Right Age

At least 18 months, but not more than 24 months.

Potty training is an important milestone for children. Most children are ready to begin potty training between the ages of 18 months and 2 years of age. However, some children will show signs of readiness before or after the average age. All children are different and will have different experiences.

Contrary to the impression that a child isn't capable of controlling his water and waste elimination until much later, current knowledge shows that the sphincter muscles which control bladder and bowel moments start developing while the baby is in utero and reach their FULL maturity between 12 – 24 months with 18 as the average. This is when toileting should be COMPLETED, not started. When parents start potty training AFTER these muscles reach full maturity, the muscles have become limp from not having the opportunity of practicing eliminating. It is our job as parents to provide these practice opportunities and respond to these cues as soon as possible.

18

You may start noticing readiness signs at that age, "where a lot of toddlers start to show an interest in the potty or toilet." Pediatricians agree that most children have a "window" when training is most easily completed. For girls, this is usually between 2 and 2½ years of age, and for boys, between 2½ and 3, after which children can become attached to diapers, develop problem behaviours, or at least reject potty training.

New parents may have the impression that the earlier a child is introduced to the potty, the longer the actual training, but this is not so. The best results are for those who start training from 19 months to 24 months. On average, these children are out of diapers by 25 months.

Among the parents who waited until their child was between two and three, some trained quickly and others took much longer than those in the 19- to 24-month group because the training period coincided with the "terrible twos."

If you see that a child is clearly not ready to start potty training, then don't force him to. There may be other conditions present that are causing stress and resistance. As soon as the first sign of emotional distress shows up in the child, it is time to stop for at least a month, then try to approach potty training in a different way. But as long as the child is cooperative and parents are willing to make an effort, it will be successful.

No such thing as a specific age to begin potty training

The transition from diapers to underwear will be much smoother if you react to a child's awareness, rather than be fixed on a specific age. Potty-training success hinges on physical and emotional readiness. It's up to us parents to recognize this, and not to pressure a child to do something he is not ready for yet.

Chapter 4: Knowing When to Start

Remember how exciting it was to finally learn how to ride a bicycle for the first time, and move up from the 3- or 4-wheeled version? That's a bit of how it feels to move from diapers to using the potty. It may seem out of reach for a while, then a bit wobbly, then a wonder when it finally happens.

Each child shows readiness at different periods than others, within that window of time most conducive to potty training. Younger siblings may take to it quicker when they want to imitate their older brother or sister, or slower if the time of training happens to coincide with a stressful period in the family. But the important thing is for us parents to be able to recognize when a child is READY.

Many parents repeatedly acknowledge they do not know how to detect the signs of child readiness. Here are several of the usual signs that your child is ready for potty-training:

✓ Seems interested in the potty chair or toilet.

✓ Is becoming interested in watching others go to the toilet (this can be awkward or make you uncomfortable at first, but is a good way to introduce things).

✓ This can include watching you potty, asking questions regarding the toilet or sitting on the potty.

✓ Showing an interest in the toilet when someone else is using it. General readiness skills, even when not yet interested in the toilet.

✓ Able to walk and sit down on his own for short periods of time.

✓ Can sit on and rise from a potty chair.

✓ Can stabilize himself with his feet so he can push when he's having a bowel movement.

✓ Imitates his parents around the house.

✓ Begins to show a desire to please parents or carers.

✓ Can put things back in their place.

✓ Shows understanding about things having their place around the home.

✓ Is becoming generally more independent when it comes to completing tasks.

✓ Desire to be autonomous.

✓ Has dry diapers for up to two hours. This shows he's able to store pee in his bladder (which automatically empties in younger babies or newborns).

Able to communicate his or her wants

✓ Not even through words yet, but through bodily movements, looks, facial expressions, hand gestures.

✓ Can understand and follow basic directions, such as 'Give the ball to daddy.'

✓ Understands words used for elimination.

✓ Tells you (or shows obvious signs) when he does a poo or pee in his diaper, or about to.

✓ So it's important for parents to learn how the child communicates. It may begin with physical discomfort, which turns into wriggles and squirms, then small sounds and words, which is communication, pre-language.

Uncomfortable with wet or soiled diapers

✓ Complains about wet or dirty diapers, or does actions like pulling off diaper and peeing on the floor.

✓ Signals that his or her diaper is wet or soiled. A child needs to be wet and feel wet and uncomfortable to realize they need to go to the potty and tell you when they need to go.

✓ May even ask to be changed when diaper is soiled, or try to scoop out poo from his diaper.

✓ Starts to be conscious that a diaper is about to be wet, looking down at it before he pees.

✓ Sometimes even asking to wear underwear or refusing to put on a diaper.

✓ May even be able to pull down his or her pants and pull them up again with little or no assistance.

Not all these signs need to be present when your child is ready. Most children show even just one or two of these signs. A general trend will let you know it's time to start.

Again, if your child has recently faced or is about to face a major change, such as moving house or the arrival of a new sibling, it is best to wait awhile before actual training. A toddler who opposes potty training today will be more willing after a month.

Relax and know that development doesn't happen overnight. It is a process and takes time and practice to see desirable results.

To understand how soon a child will be ready to start potty training, we take a look at two development theories. These represent contrasting views on both ends of the spectrum.

Child-Centered Training

This theory was first advocated in the 1960s and revolves around the fact that toilet training is completely dependent on the child. Parents are there to guide but are never encouraged to push their child to begin potty training. They can look for signs and give their child many opportunities to use the toilet, but they should never force them into using it. With this idea, potty training may not happen until the child turns four or when he is ready.

Advocating for Diaper-less babies

Before the 1950s, diapers weren't used as often as they are today. Many advocates have observed that older generations started potty training earlier. They were more in tune to their elimination needs and sensations that go with it. When they pinpointed the cues and body language of their child, they would set him over the toilet and make sounds such as "sss" or say "pee-pee." The child learns to go about his business through active conditioning.

The best takeaway from these two different theories is that the combination of them produces the best results. The first child-centred approach gives credit to the child's feelings and independence. But without a guide to give that little push, you may be holding out on training for a much longer time as intended. By then, it may well be too late to start. The second theory relies on conditioning the small child over the toilet regardless of his needs. The best way to approach this is somewhere in the middle of these two theories.

Between the age of 18 months to three years, your child will reach the point of muscle control that makes it possible for self-regulation. You can enhance the chances of him succeeding in his potty-training journey at around 18-24 months old. Other indicators, such as the cues and his interest in using the potty, will prompt you to start. It is important that you watch for the signs of readiness.

Keep tabs on your child's elimination habits. After a meal, take note of how long it takes for him to pee or have a bowel movement. When you start potty-training, this knowledge of timing can be useful to lead him to his potty chair. When you can time the bathroom moment when he is very likely feeling the urge, then you can expect far better results. With this method, you are also trying to figure out when he will need to go so that you can sit him on the potty and do the deposit in the bowl instead of the diaper.

Elimination control can happen in stages and this is the order in which it occurs:

Night-time bowel control > Daytime bowel control > Daytime bladder control > Night-time bladder control

Takeaway: Toilet Training Checklist

There are some benchmarks that the child can clear faster than others. The list below shows some of the most common behaviours your child exhibits when he is ready to be potty trained. Keep in mind that all children are different, and yours may have other ways of letting you know. He may mature at a different pace or may have a greater tolerance for being soiled. Use your common sense and knowledge about your child as you know him best. It is not necessary for him to achieve all the things in the checklist before you can start the toilet training:

1. Your child stays dry after naps or at least 2 hours at a time during the day.

2. Regular and more predictable bowel movements begin.

3. Telling signs when your child is about to urinate or have a bowel movement through facial expressions, posture or words.

4. Your child is able to follow simple instructions.

5. Your child is able to walk to and from the bathroom and can help in undressing himself.

27

6. Your child begins to feel uncomfortable wearing soiled diapers and wants a change.

7. Your child begins to ask for a potty chair or use the toilet.

8. Your child wants to wear grown-up underwear.

Chapter 5: Preparing Yourself

Most parents eagerly look forward to potty training as a sort of D-day in their child's development. The end to changing diapers is in sight! But many daddies and mommies don't want to think of the effort it will take. Besides, who wants to think about that? But anything done without thoughtful and considerate effort is responded to without pleasure.

We need to both lay down the basic training, and to follow up the basics with practice. Yes, some children get it within a few days while some take several months. We need to be prepared for how long it can take. Promise, it will be worth all the effort, and not as long as we think.

Here's one way not to do it, and yet how we often do: A new baby is on the way. Our family and friends get so excited they travel long distances to surround us with love and concern, each one shooting their own arrows of advice at us. The fact that their own children are just regular rebels and not the cherubs they make them out to be seems like a minor detail. When our baby is born, we marvel at every wonder, take in every moment.

Then we wait for that perfect hour. We're armed and ready with equipment. We visualize just how it's going to be, a potty-training storyboard with maybe a bit of drama, a lot of humor, and a definite happy ending. Then on the appointed day, we bring out the potty, expecting him to clap and smile. But when they don't, we crumple inwardly. They don't like it, push it away, cry at the sight of it. What did I do wrong?

After the dust has settled, and we get over our disappointment that we failed even if we prepared everything, we suddenly remember that we overlooked the first, most important sign to consider: our child's readiness to learn.

Potty-training is not just a chore we slot into the calendar, like three days of camping, or repainting the kitchen, or redoing chores that we asked someone else to do. Once we decide on the three days we are to potty-train, the first one really being trained is us—parents. We learn to read the signs of our child about when they are going to eliminate or pass water.

When we approach potty-training as a vital part of good health, just like eating, believe it or not, you can actually relax. You can take a relaxed approach to teaching. You won't have to worry. Being relaxed is one of the things you can do to make your child's transition from diapers to the potty a stress-free experience. You can relax once you:

✓ let go of expectations.

✓ let go of comparing the present potty-trainee. with other children, even our own other children.

✓ know how your child's body and mind work.

✓ recognize signs of readiness.

✓ decide when and how to start potty-training.

✓ know how to talk about potty training with your child.

✓ determine how to adapt the 3-day method in a manner that's best for your child and your family.

✓ know what problems and setbacks to expect.

✓ consider how you were potty-trained.

Be involved in all areas of your child's learning

Before introducing the potty, it helps a lot if you have an established daily routine with your child in other learning activities. This way, the new method of using the potty can be introduced into your normal routine without being a strange, sudden phase that could frighten instead of interest them.

Children still need to know what is expected of them. If done in a considerate and interactive way, you do your child much good by providing direction and expectations, while also considering their readiness. Some children really are ready to be trained early, so you are not 'pushing' if you are meeting no resistance. Their resistance could be one of your cues. Children really do love learning from the way grown ups do things, so don't deny them their opportunity if it fits their readiness.

Start potty training only when you and your child are ready

Your child may be ready, but what about you? Do you have more than you can handle in your job? Have you just given birth to another baby? When you perceive your child is ready, you must also examine if you are willing to devote the three full days for helping your child through the process of learning to use the potty. You need to be ready as your child is to find the right fit for the 3-day method.

Prepare to give up all your regular activities for 3 days in a row

Don't schedule potty-training during a time where your attention is taken up by large demands, such as moving to a new house or expecting a new baby. It's best to wait until things have settled down a bit, or resumed a regular routine, so both you and your child can have the time and good humor to deal with setbacks and surprises. Arrange for stand-ins, substitute help/cooperation for daily chores/activities during thosethree days. But inform the people who come to help you, or other family members that you won't be able to chat and converse like as usual, because you will need to focus on the child being trained. It's very important that nothing diverts your attention, so that you are able to catch EACH time your child needs to pee or poo.

Choose three days where you have no obligations, or cancel any obligations you do have. A long peekend is ideal. If you have other children, find babysitters for them if you can or plan to occupy them with TV for most of the day. Make meals ahead of time for those 3 days or budget money for eating out.

Decide on the vocabulary

Make sure everyone in the family, eventually daycare workers or teachers, follow the same routine and use the same names for body parts and bathroom acts. Let them know how you're handling the issue and ask that they use the same approaches so your child won't become confused.

Prepare to dedicate your time and energy to the child

You are ready to potty train when you can devote the time and energy necessary to encourage your child on a daily basis. Remember that you may have to approach this child differently from your other children, depending on how you read the signals and movements. Girls are definitely different from boys. And even one daughter takes to the training in a different way than another. If it clicks faster with one, but takes longer with another, that's just the way it is.

Don't go back to diapers when the going gets rough

Potty training is messy and a kid wetting themselves is something they'll get over. You just have to plough on through with using regular underwear and not resort to trainer pants or pull-ups because then it can become confusing for the child. As long as they take interest in the process, you can always wipe up a pee puddle or patches of poo and know that it will click with them eventually.

Learn how a child signals their need to pee or poo

When you notice signs that your child might need to use the potty — such as a change in facial expression, squirming, squatting or holding the genital area – respond quickly.

Help your child to become familiar with these signals, stop what he or she is doing and head to the potty. Praise your child for telling you when he or she has to go. When it's time to flush, let your child do the honors. Make sure your child washes his or her hands after using the potty.

Some parents try the method of putting the child on the potty chair, even if they have not signalled a need to go. Or you might notice that your child uses her bowels at a certain time of the day, so you would probably try putting her on the potty at this time. This doesn't work for all children, and I personally don't recommend it – true potty training begins when the child is aware of the sensation of doing a pee or poo and connects this with getting to the potty in time. So it is much better to wait till the actual moment of needing to pee or poo to go to the potty.

If possible, don't involve multiple people in actual potty training

If husband or grandma helps, make sure you both use the same words and terms for things so it doesn't confuse the child. But still, it is more ideal for the parent who has seen the readiness signs and has established constant rapport with the child to be the one to do the training.

Nursing mothers can still potty-train another child, if you have reached a regular routine with the new baby. The potty-trainee will be glad to help you with the baby. Then if he needs to go, stop nursing the baby and respond to the needs of the child being potty-trained.

During moments that try your patience, remember motivating reasons for potty-training, such as: "A few days of frustration and cleaning up constant accidents is far better than a few more months of changing dirty, smelly diapers."

Chapter 6: Preparing the Child

In addition to understanding the bodily sensations, getting to the bathroom and getting clothes off, a child must first constrict sphincter muscles to achieve control, and then relax them to eliminate. Obviously there is a lot to learn. Gaining bowel and bladder control is a skill and fortunately, children usually like to learn new skills.

The usual sequence for these skills are: First comes bowel regularity, followed by bowel control. Daytime bladder control often comes next but for many children this can happen simultaneously, and finally, later comes nighttime bladder control.

Start to teach potty-training words

When you decide that it is time to begin potty training, there are some things you can do to make the transition from diapers to underwear smoother. Teach your child some words associated with going to the potty – for example, you might want to teach her words like 'pee,' 'poo' and 'I need to go.' Before actual potty training, start responding to child's bowel movements with words that express "how yucky it is to poop in the diaper." Be definite about this. Talk them through (pulling down pants, sitting, pooping, peeing, flushing, washing hands) over and over. Make it 'normal.'

Begin to make diaper-changing tedious

Once the child begins to show discomfort with a soiled diaper, try to make changing their diaper just as much of a chore for them as it is for you, so that using the potty will seem easier in comparison. Begin to show your child what regular child underwear (not padded version) looks like. If using cloth diapers, this isn't necessary, as the child understands the feeling of wetness or soiling much earlier.

A child won't learn to be dry if kept in disposable diapers, as it doesn't let a child feel wet. Once the child stops wearing disposables and starts with underwear, it takes a while for him to understand and dislike the feeling of wetting and how to recognise those feelings before they pee on the floor.

Familiarize your child with the bathroom/toilet

A couple of weeks before actual 3-day potty training, allow your child to be present when you go to the bathroom so that your child will feel comfortable in the bathroom.

Introduce an activity like reading a fun potty-training book or having a special toy to use while sitting on the potty chair. Stay with your child when he or she is in the bathroom.

Even if your child simply sits there, offer praise even for trying. Allow your child to watch others who are using the toilet, and talk about what they're doing.

Have them bunch up the toilet paper and use a new piece of bunched up toilet paper for each wipe.

When you're done with the toilet, have them flush the toilet for you, waving bye-bye to the poop. Allow your child to see urine and bowel movements in the toilet. Let your child practice flushing the toilet.

Introduce the potty chair

It's good to make the potty chair available early on, because once you start the training, he already knows what the potty is for.

And if follow-up training extends into the first stages of being verbal and coordinated, it can be easier, rather than if that's the time you start.

It is ideal to put a child't potty chair in the bathroom, and not in just any other place or playing area in the house, such as the nursery, living room, or out in the garden. In a multi-storey house, put a potty in the bathrooms that your child will normally use.

You might want to try a potty chair model with a removable top that can be placed directly on the toilet later when your child is ready. Encourage your child to sit on the potty chair — with or without a diaper. Make sure your child's feet rest firmly on the floor or a stool. Help your child understand how to talk about the bathroom using simple, correct terms. You might dump the contents of a dirty diaper into the potty chair to show its purpose.

Make your child's potty a comfortable and welcoming place

One week before the actual 3-day potty training process, place the potty chair in a well-lit bathroom that is easily accessible for your child. A potty place should be a happy place.

Allow your child to observe, touch and become familiar with the potty chair. Tell your child that the potty chair is his or her own chair. Introduce and explain the potty, allowing your child to try it out for size and get familiar with it.

Encourage your child to use his potty whenever he feels the urge to go. Reassure him that he can tell you too, if he needs to go, and that you'll take him to the bathroom whenever he wants you to.

If your child is hesitant or reluctant to use the potty, don't force it. Perhaps you planned when to do potty-training, but some stressful things suddenly come up, spoiling your initial plans. So, instead of being relaxed and natural, potty-training becomes tense and hurried. If this happens, reschedule the 3-day period, and your child will regain interest when conditions are no longer stressful.

Schedule potty breaks

During the two weeks before actual 3-day potty training, sit your child on the potty only when you feel he is going to pee or have a bowel movement. There may be patterns like 30 minutes after eating or after having a bath, but these should only be guides. Don't take him to the potty if he isn't showing signs of needing to go.

It may help to show your child where his bowel movements go, even while still in diapers, shortly before the actual 3-day potty-training. Show your child how the potty chair is used. The next time he goes in his diaper, take him to his potty, sit him down, and empty the diaper beneath him into the potty. This will help him make the connection between sitting and producing, and help him understand the purpose of the potty chair.

After you've emptied his potty into the big toilet, let him flush it if he wants to (but don't make him do it if he's scared) so he can see where it goes. It is not advised to have child sit fully-clothed on the potty chair, so that they will understand the connection.

For boys, it's normal if they start urinating sitting down, and then move to standing up after bowel training is complete, or when they want to imitate their dad or older brothers. Experience has proven that it doesn't do much good to sit a child on the potty when he doesn't need to go. It's best not to make your child sit on the potty for long periods of time, because this will feel like punishment and not relief.

Install a low step/stool by the sink so the child can reach a low faucet.

Teach your child how to wash her hands after using the toilet. Make it a habit to ask if he has washed his hands and guide him using water and soap as you talk them through. This can be a fun activity that your child enjoys as part of the routine.

Chapter 7: Equipment and Supplies

If potty training occurs between 9-15 months, then you may refer to the signs of readiness stated in the previous chapter. Take it as an adventurous challenge, rather than a daunting task at hand. When you decide that it's time to potty train your child, the first thing you need to do is to train your patience. Focus on your child and on the training itself.

Preparing the area and Equipment

Choose an area of the house where you will potty train your child. This may be your bathroom, living room or the kitchen.

When it comes to equipment, get a potty or a seat that you put on top of a regular toilet seat. The first option is more common and is a great way to introduce the toilet by presenting a smaller, less intimidating version of it. Some potty seats can come in many different colours and are customizable. You may want to let your child decorate it with stickers or drawings so that he is comfortable in its presence.

This will be a good companion of your child so make sure he gets acquainted with it.

The second option allows for a more gradual transition. At this age, children will be so eager to please and take part, so there should be little resistance to toilet use. Make sure there is a little footrest with the seat for your child to use. A sturdy stool on the side can also help, especially when your child doesn't have the coordination to climb up and down the seat yet. Encourage independence but be there to guide your child.

Other equipment and things you may want to consider are a timer, clean underpants, your child's favourite toys and games, sketchpads, crayons, colouring books, a waterproof mattress pad, and stickers. Tell your kid that using the potty like a grown-up is an important part of life and make it a reason to celebrate.

Have all supplies ready before you start the actual three days of learning to use the potty.

High-fiber food supplies and lots of liquids

More than they normally drink in a day. Water is best and a variety of other fruit liquids.

Potty chair

Bring the child along and let them choose the potty they like.

There are many advantages to using a potty chair before shifting to the kind of trainer seat that fits securely inside the existing toilet seat. You can take the potty chair anywhere, even on the road, and can become a familiar presence, and some children find it friendlier than a toilet. Try to find out your child's preference and go with that.

Eventually, the child will learn to use both the potty and the toilet.

Take your child to the store with you, sit on different potties and pick the potty the child wants. If he can manage, let him carry it out of the store, to the car and set it up themselves in the bathroom.

Real underwear

Have 20 to 30 pairs on hand. Bring your child along to pick out big kid underpants.

AVOID the padded version of trainer pants or pull-ups. As part of building up the excitement, go on a small shopping trip on the week before the actual 3-day training, allow your child to choose a few packs of big kid underwear. Often, a child who has an idea what underwear is will get excited about seeing big boy/big girl cotton pieces with their favorite cartoon character on them.

This 3-day method of potty training shifts from diapers straight to real underwear, no pull-ups or trainer pants as a potty-training aid, as pull-ups just encourage children to pee in them.

Disposable training pants are marketed as a soft-intro to real underwear, but it's just not as effective. Training pants may seem convenient at first, prevent messes from getting on floors, couches, precious surfaces but they confuse children and make them think it is okay to use them like diapers. But training pants only slows down the potty-training process.

Pull-ups are also another type of product that cause more delay. They have long been ridiculed on the grounds that they prevent the child from sensing moisture from accidents, thereby delaying potty-training. What's worse is that they are often marketed as underwear for 3-4 year olds who are not yet potty-trained, postponing body skills even further.

Easy-wear clothing

Make sure your child's wardrobe is adaptable to potty training. In other words, avoid overalls and shirts with several snaps or fasteners. Simple clothes are a must at this stage and kids who are potty training need to be able to undress themselves easily.

Moist bathroom wipes

You can have them in the bathroom for a couple of days so your child knows those are big people wipes.

Moist wipes offers a cleaner, easier and more gentle clean than dry toilet paper. However, most baby wipes and bathroom wipes are made of non-biodegradable material and cannot be flushed down the toilet, and do not decompose. There are alternative flushable moist wipes available, but they still contain ingredients found in household soap, which may cause irritation when it comes in contact with the eyes.

There are also healthier alternatives to commercially-produced moist wipes. Many mothers regularly convert a roll of paper towels into 2 rolls of moist wipes by soaking the material in a mixture of water, baby wash, and baby oil/almond oil. They then store the moist paper wipes in an airtight container, a roll usually lasts about 4 - 8 weeks, and also stay moist. When you calculate the cost, it's very economical and you can customize the scent.

Others make their own homemade cloth baby wipes, which are reusable. Though the idea can sound strange to those accustomed to disposable wipes, it certainly saves money and has the least environmental impact. Making cloth baby wipes out of the best available material will cost less than $60 for a set of 24 that will last you from birth to potty training. Traditional wipes run about $4 for a pack of 80, but may last only a week, running up an expense of around $208 per year!

People choose to make their own baby wipes so they know exactly what is in the solution and what is touching their baby's bottom. Instead of alcohol, perfume and chlorine commonly found in traditional moist wipes, homemade wipes are soaked in the same natural substances as the moist paper wipes, and are the most nurturing, and the least irritating to your child's skin.

Snacks, treats, rewards

Devise a reward system that matches your parenting style, and doesn't clash with what your child is used to from you.

For example, you may purchase a gift bag with your child's favorite cartoon character and fill it with 'pee' prizes or 'poo' prizes. Coloring books, small toys, and single Hershey's Kisses are examples of some of the items. When your child goes poo, she gets to pick a prize. If she gets to pee, you could use stickers and fruit snacks.

For many potty-training, Mini M&M's helps a lot. The system could be, each time your kid goes potty, he gets two or three, but if he wipes himself (which is a huge achievement) then he gets four or five. This helps a child overcome that difficult part where he doesn't want to poo because the part about learning how to wipe is kind of yucky.

If your child responds to stickers or stars on a chart, you could use that as well. A reward chart can be a helpful tool to use in which the child can see a visual reminder of how good they are doing. Some parents choose to reward their child with a special book, toy or other item when the child has stayed dry or used the potty for a certain amount of time.

For others, trips to the park or extra bedtime stories are effective. Experiment to find what works best for your child.

Reinforce your child's effort with verbal praise, such as, "This is great! You're learning to use the potty just like big kids do!" Even if your child doesn't do a complete routine successfully, give praise about any part of the process that he is able to do.

Feeding for Success

Choosing the right area and potty is one thing, but since potty training is all about elimination, you can make the experience easier by helping your child eat the right food. Amp up the likelihood of your child being in a frame of mind of eliminating by increasing fibre and water intake. Here are some stool-softening foods you can try out: peaches, pear nectar, apricots, berries, plums, prune juice, grapes, vegetables, or apple juice. Try to stay away from food that tends to constipate or harden stool such as white bread, cheese, excessive milk, or pasta.

Cleaning supplies

You'll also want to have supplies for cleaning up accidents, such as rags, cleaning solution, and a plastic bucket.

Chapter 8: The Gameplan

Once everything is ready to go, it is now time to prime up your child's mindset. You can tell him that you will be organizing a potty party for him and that all his toys will be attending. Explain the importance of doing the training and that it is an important part of him being a big boy and growing up. You can try to show him colourful underwear and ask him to try it on. Some parents recommend that during potty training, the child should stay naked from the waist down. But this is unnecessary, and you can do without this step.

For the first few weeks, start the day with a visit to the potty as soon as he wakes up. Make this a daily morning ritual. Walk to his room, pull up the curtains, throw him a big good morning kiss, then declare, "It's time to wake up and go to the toilet." This way, you are not asking your child's opinion, but stating it as a fact of life. By leaving out his choice, you are making the act as normal as telling him it's time to brush his teeth. Do not ask, just do it.

He may have peed during the night, so the diaper may still be wet, and he may not want to pee again. Sit him in the potty for no more than 5 minutes. Hold his hand and get comfortable by telling a story, singing a song, or talking about his day ahead. Make it a pleasant experience each time. If he does urinate, associate it with yourself by saying, "Oh look, you're peeing the way Mommy does. That's great!" Children at this age want to imitate Mom and Dad. This will give him the encouragement he needs. Once he is done, show your child how to wipe himself clean. This is the same for both genders, whether it's peeing or pooping. Little girls should be taught to wipe front to back. They may struggle and not get it right immediately, so be prepared to have all hands on deck. You might have to do it yourself. But if you do, talk your child through what you are doing. Make sure they understand the importance of cleaning up after themselves.

For little boys, he may get an erection while sitting on the potty. At this stage, try not to teach him to pee standing up yet. He has to nail peeing and pooping while sitting down first before you can teach him how to stand and aim.

If your child is unable to pee, take him off the potty. Put on a new diaper and give him breakfast. Around 20 minutes after your child drinks liquids, put him on the potty again and repeat the process. Do this for the rest of the day, after he drinks or when you think he will have another bowel movement again. Some children pee or poo right before a bath. If this applies to your child, take the opportunity to toilet train him again.

For the first few weeks, go slowly but remain consistent. Try to avoid placing your child on the potty for only once a day. This can be confusing for the child, who may end up thinking that the potty is only used after breakfast or before taking a bath. Help your child develop his senses by keeping him in touch with his bodily functions and sensations. Make him see the connection between elimination and sitting on the toilet or potty. He may still have incomplete control over his sphincter muscles. Provide him with the opportunity to recognize these sensations and practice control. This will make the transition as smooth as possible.

Always remember that your child will learn everything within a week or two. It's a common myth to "learn potty training in 3 days." Do not give up or feel frustrated when it seems to take longer than you expect. The more supportive you are, the more likely your child will want to succeed.

Establishing the Steps

When giving verbal instructions, keep in mind that you have to go as slow as you possibly can. Allow your child to take in the information, and carefully explain each step from sitting down to flushing.

A child learns best when being shown what to do, so you may tell him, "Watch how I pull down my pants. Now, let's see you try it. Then let's see you climb on the potty, just to see how fun it is!" For the child to feel like a self-starter, that's a good thing.

Next, talk about how when one sits on the potty, that's where your poop or pee goes. You may use examples of his older brothers or sisters, or the toilet for mommy and daddy. Explain to him in an enthusiastic way how toddlers like him are moving up to training pants to use the potty and that it's such an important milestone in a growing boy.

Next, show your child how to wipe himself clean. You may hold off teaching him this step once he has fully learned how to eliminate inside the potty. There is no rush but show him that it is important to clean himself up after he does his business. Once he moves on to toilet training, you can then teach him to flush. Try to make it fun, but explain to him that toilets aren't toys, and these are the types of bathroom equipment one shouldn't play with. If your child voices out concern about falling inside the toilet, tell him that it may be big enough to hold his poop and toilet paper, but not large enough to swallow him whole. Do not bore him with detailed explanations on plumbing – just keep it light and fun in terms he will understand. When it comes to diaper disposal, talk to him about how his toys all belong in a particular box or space and that his poop should have a designated place for it as well. Your child may react to this in many different ways. Some may be interested or even fascinated by the idea, and some may feel scared or anxious about the sudden disappearing act. Take your cue on how to respond by listening and watching for his reactions to this step. This will help you learn to readjust your training accordingly. Also, avoid shaming him by making statements like, "Your poop is really stinky today" or "You really dirtied your diaper." These statements will make your child feel as though he has done something naughty and is a cause for embarrassment. It does not help with the potty-training process as he will interpret going to the toilet as an act of shame instead. Don't make him feel funny about dropping his poop and pee in hollow spaces.

Lastly, show him how to wash up his hands by singing the Happy Birthday song while his hands are being lathered with warm water and soap. Teach him that learning to use the potty is only as successful as knowing how to keep himself clean afterward.

Handling a Job Well Done

Every time your child uses the potty, give him a small reward of any sort. Make sure to explain and tell him what the reward is for and why you are giving it to him. He will learn to associate potty training with a positive outlook.

Positive feedback can help reinforce any desirable behaviour. Be extra careful with how you phrase out your words since it can make or break your child's determination to learn potty training in time. Some good lines that help send the message across are the following:

- ✓ "You got to the potty in time – that's really good of you!"

- ✓ "You're really getting better at taking off your pants down all by yourself."

- ✓ "You're doing awesome at using the potty – you won't be needing any help form grown-ups in no time."

- ✓ "You're doing a great job at flushing the toilet all by yourself."

Make your child feel that she's the star of the whole process. You are only there to guide, coach, and teach her, but without her cooperation, both of you are going nowhere. Your goal is to help her listen to the signs her body makes when a pee or poop is coming on. Tell her that when she squats or sits down, or feel a tingling sensation or pressure, those signals mean she has to go the toilet because a BM is coming on. There will be times when she's in her diaper and she's already pooped or peed in it before telling you. Explain to her that she needs to tell you just before the action happens and that you will be there to guide her throughout.

When to lose the Diaper

When your child is able to keep himself dry during the day for a week, you may begin to make the switch to underwear. Disposable pull-ups feel too much like diapers as they do not allow the child to feel wet for a prolonged time. For night-time control, it usually takes much longer to train. Try not to leave a diaper off while sleeping until he has woken up dry for at least two weeks.

Many parents tend to have much fewer questions regarding night-time training as opposed to daytime training. Once daytime training becomes established, night-time dryness tends to follow naturally.

Children tend to follow and model big-people behaviour. With this in mind, give heaps of praise and lots of enthusiasm when you prime his mindset for potty training. Show him examples and illustrations of bigger children, school-age children who wear pants without diapers. Or point out the same-sex role model for your child (fathers for boys, mothers for girls) and suggest that if they want to start acting like a grown-up, then they should dress the part as well. Take this enlightened approach instead of forcing upon your child the need for potty training, and you will reap successful results.

Potty Training for Boys

Potty training boys should start at two years old or older. It is also better to train peeing and pooping by sitting down before he can practice aiming and peeing standing up. Once the initial phase of sitting down is over and executed well, the help of male role models can come into play. Fathers, grandfathers, older brothers, or uncles can step in to show your child exactly what to do. Parents of the opposite sex can also talk the child through the differences between girls and boys. Explain to him why they differ when it comes to eliminating.

Make a game out of aiming while eliminating. Having a target practice may be quite helpful, as this will improve their eye-body coordination. You can set up some Hula Hoops snacks or Cheerios in your little boy's potty. Perhaps place a ping pong ball inside the toilet for him to aim at. You can also make the experience more exciting by adding blue dye (food colouring) to the water in the toilet. When your little boy pees, seeing the colour of the water change will pique his interest.

Do not forget to reward your child with every successful step. Boys tend to be prouder than girls, so do not show your anger or disappointment when he hasn't figured out the aiming part. Bear in mind what his character and quirks are, and tailor your methods to this.

Potty Training for Girls

Girls are usually potty-trained earlier than boys. Girls tend to be more particular about hygiene than boys. As with regular potty training, allow her to sit on the potty first. Teach your little girl how to wipe the right way from the front to the back. This prevents bringing germs from the anal region to the vaginal opening, which can lead to urinary tract infections. Keep in mind that if girls wear diapers for far too long, it can increase the risk of developing a bladder infection. Entice her with underwear that is brightly coloured with cute designs. Allow her to choose the design she wants so that she will feel more responsible and more adult-like. This will encourage her to use the potty more to wear cute underwear.

Understanding Day and Night Training

Day wetting and night-time wetting may seem the same, but they are two different sides of the same coin. Each needs to be handled and trained differently.

If your child wets his bed in his sleep, it can mean two things. This is either because he hasn't acquired the bladder control development needed to keep himself dry in his sleep or he hasn't completely made the association between sensation and method of execution. If daytime wetting occurs, it may be because your child became too preoccupied with his toys to not notice that he needs to go and pee. This slip-up should clear out in a week or two, especially if he has already been potty trained.

As your child's body develops, his bladder capacity also tends to increase. Most kids have trouble at night, and it is more common than day wetting. This is because your child hasn't gotten used to the bigger bladder capacity, although he can use it to hold pee in longer.

Daytime wetting is unusual in kids older than five years old. Your child may experience daytime peeing when running, playing, or in some little girls, giggling. Some children also have a lazy bladder, wherein they pee every 8 or 9 hours only and have several pee accidents between. In this instance, the child doesn't get the sensation of having a full bladder, and that's when the accidents happen. As a parent, have him go to the toilet several times a day and keep reminding him to do so even if there is no urge. Doctors will usually give medical treatment for a lazy bladder, as it is often accompanied by constipation and bladder infections now and then. Promote complete emptying even though your little tot is in a hurry to get back to the playground.

By medical definition, the term bedwetting applies to children who are five years old and above but still wet their beds in their sleep. While your initial reaction may be one of shock and dismay, your child may feel embarrassed as well. He may even feel guilty about it and may dread owning up to you. The experience might be disturbing for him, so show as much understanding and support as you can. Try to figure out the possible reasons why he might be wetting his bed. He may have a bladder that is maturing late; something that is physical in nature and will usually resolve itself by waiting out a few more months. If this occurs beyond five years, have the problem checked with a physician to rule out any medical conditions or illnesses. Another reason may be due to the slowpoke syndrome, which allows the slow maturing of the central nervous system. This is generally associated with night-time pee. The message that the bladder is full fails to reach his brain, and thus the control of his bladder is absent.

There might be the presence of a pee-prone gene pool. Some kids may also have low night-time levels of antidiuretic hormone, which prevents the production of urine. If this hormone is low, then night-time wetting is most likely to occur – and often. The good news is that this can easily be remedied by medication. Bedwetting can also be a response to stress. This is fairly common and can be alleviated once the stressor is removed or has passed. Children who have experienced abuse often bed wet, which contributes to a vicious cycle of shame and low self-esteem. If you have recently adopted a child, look for signs of emotional distress.

Night-Time Bedwetting

What should you do about night-time bedwetting? Here are a few solutions which can help you out.

Remind your child to take a pee before he goes to bed. Plan this pre-bed potty trip so that his bladder gets emptied before sleeping.

Limit the amount of fluids he takes before going to bed. Make sure he avoids drinks that are chock-full of aspartame and caffeine.

Try to do timed wakeups. You may feel guilty about your child not getting enough sleep, but this is vital to solve the night-time peeing problem. If you practice waking him up at the same time every night, it will become an automatic habit. Go with him but allow him to lead you towards the potty.

Make sure he sleeps in a comfortable and conducive space for rest. Place the potty near him or rearrange his bed, so that the toilet is accessible when he gets up. Make everything very easy and safe to access.

Expect slip-ups to happen. It will take some time to overcome bedwetting. Provide sleeping spot protection such as placing a mattress protector underneath. Consider also having a bed cover made of rubber or plastic. Make sure there is a ready supply of fresh sheets and underwear handy.

Night clothes should be easy to take off during the night when he wants to go. If your child decides that it is too much work to take off his pyjamas, then he may resort to wetting the bed instead.

Try to keep your family a safe haven from teasing about constant bedwetting. Make it clear to those around him that making a big deal out of bedwetting is wrong. This can have a psychological toll which is less than desirable.

As tempting as it may be, do not switch back to using diapers. This sends a signal to your child that you're giving up on him. While lapses can be a pain, try not to over-react and revert back to diapers. He may follow suit and give up too.

Chapter 9: How to deal with Potential Issues

Remember that accidents do happen. Stay calm and hold your temper. This can be hard to do, especially when you see your carpet or floor in a mess. Take a deep breath and remember that this is temporary. If an accident like this does happen, tell your child to change his wet underwear and put on a clean, dry one in a calm voice. Once your child becomes involved in this process, he will learn about responsibility and realise the mistake he has made. Be casual about accidents, taking care not to be over-concerned. Be careful not to point out little mistakes as your child will feel like a failure even with a little smirk or frown. Sooner or later, he will get into the groove, unless you're always there pushing too hard.

Backsliding and Regressing

The most common issue when it comes to potty training is backsliding. A blip in the otherwise smooth ride has made you think twice about whether he has mastered the whole process.

But your child is a child after all, and you cannot allow stress to make you act like you only approve of him only when he's doing well. Showing that you are stressed reflects the stress to your child. It is counterproductive to make him feel guilty. So, what is the best way to handle this little accident?

Right after the accident occurs, clean and wash him up, and put on a fresh set of underpants. Then, sit him on top of the potty. Make him understand that he doesn't need to go now, but that you want him to practice sitting there. Tell him that the next time he wants to go, he can tell you, so that you can assist him in getting to the potty in time. Keep mentioning how much he likes doing things on his own. Talk to him about the specific details such as the sensations he gets to feel when a pee or poop is coming. Keep it simple, and keep it clear about the things you want him to recognise and do. Pinpoint if there were stressors that made him regress and forget about the task at hand. Did you have to make adjustments to a new home, a new job, illness, or is there anything else that's disrupting your daily routine as a family? If everything seems to be going well for these things, then ask yourself if your child was ready to start the toilet training. Did he show readiness? What were the signs? You may need to re-do the training all over again once you have located the source of the regression. If not, simply reinforcing should be able to get you and your child back on track.

Slow Progress

When progress is slow and erratic, you may find yourself disheartened. Don't ever show your displeasure or your child will be able to pick up on every little piece and nuance of disappointment. He may want to cooperate but is unable to control the workings of his body yet. Be supportive and his motivation will soar.

Potty training time is not a time to preach to your child. Give reminders but do not nag. If you find him with wet pants, encourage him instead of a stern scolding. Telling him to clean up his own accident will introduce a punitive element to the whole process of potty training. When it comes to these situations, do not make your child admit that he messed up.

Introducing other Caregivers

Another problem that is seen in toddlers is associating the potty process with one parent. This can lead to him refusing to use the potty unless you go with him. Early in the training, you need to set the ground rules. Tell him that peeing and pooping are his own "deal" and that he needs to do it by himself, but that you will be there to support him.

Because everyone is different, there might be a lack of consistency once he starts day care or a school for toddlers. The introduction of outside caregivers who may not be on the same page as you are can jar the training. Some of them may not understand why it's such a big deal for a child to stay consistent in his potty-training journey. Some can be overzealous in helping out. Regardless of the type of outside caregiver, you will be dealing with, it is important to bring everyone together on the same page. Day care workers may use just one approach for all the children they are looking after, and your child may not fit into that general approach. Lay out all your must-dos for your child's individualised training. After all, you are paying good money for their services. You can give out a checklist to them as guidance. You can also explain to your child what you're doing so that he will know how to cue Cousin Martha or Aunt Gina or Teacher Barbara when it's time to go potty.

Keeping Busy

Kids can get very preoccupied with playing. Even after the training phase, they can sometimes encounter a snag. They may forget or even refuse to take the time to go the potty or toilet when they are too engaged with fun activities. You can help by telling him that you haven't seen him use the bathroom in a while. Let him know that he can always go back to his toys once he goes to the toilet or potty.

Fending off Night-monsters

Once night-time use of the potty becomes a reality, you may want to ease any fears your child has of going to the bathroom by leaving a night-light around. Make it accessible so that he can reach it if he needs to. This will help dispel any night-time fears of shadows and monsters lurking in the corners.

Dealing with a Headstrong Kid

Not all kids are the same, and once in a while you can draw the short straw. You may end up with a kid who refuses to use the potty. No matter how hard you try, you can't get him to sit, much less do his business in the potty or toilet. Sure, the child is a challenge and he has a mind of his own. But that doesn't mean you should give up.

Make sure that there is nothing physical or emotional which is causing the refusal. It could be related to stress. If he is in the clear, then it could boil down to his headstrong personality. If your child's wired temperament sets him up for an argument, keep searching for management techniques that fit. Different methods exist for dealing with him – you just need to find them. A child may have tantrums as a result of attention-seeking behaviour when his parents are too busy for him. Or it can be that a parent's own irritability spills over to the child. To set aside this level of insecurity and distrust, try to set aside a week of special closeness and bonding with your child. Make that extra time for reading, playing, talking, and cuddling. You may then start to see the defiant temperament fade away. An angry child won't function well when trying to learn a new skill such as potty training. You may want to delay the potty use until she's past the troublesome issue.

Double-check your parenting reins. Sometimes, a defiant child does what he does because he feels too restricted and controlled in the other areas of his life. Handle him with the right combination of love and patience, and he should come around eventually.

If your child is in day care, try to gain some insight by talking and brainstorming with her teacher. Being with your child at home may be different from when she's at day care. With the help of the day care caregiver, you can both figure out the best approach.

Remain unfazed when dealing with the flareups. Show your child that all his tantrums are rolling off you. Keep yourself calm and do not show annoyance even when you feel like lashing back at him. Promise fun times ahead and fascinate him with big-kid places and things he can do once he's potty trained. Hold on to that lure of fascination and you may entice him to finally get himself potty trained. When he does make the choice that he's finally ready, praise him for his good judgement.

Training a child with disabilities

Depending on the disability, handling the physical aspect of a child with the problem varies. You may need to provide the right equipment for mobility, such as walkers or wheelchairs. Lessen the proximity between your child and the potty or toilet. Provide safety with bars or handrails along the sides of the toilet or bathroom to cling on to. Pad the potty or toilet seat with foam if the seat is too hard or if it becomes too cold for him. Put waterproof sheeting on so that accidents will be a lot easier to clean up afterwards. You may need a custom potty or chair, so source this out with the help of your physician. Some of the features that are modified are:

- ✓ A wheelchair with a hinged padded seat in the centre that can be lowered to become a commode chair.

- ✓ A manual wheelchair that can be lowered to be converted into a commode to fit a standard toilet.

- ✓ A self-inflating cushion to assist the child with moving from his wheelchair to the toilet or potty.

- ✓ Grab bars on each side of the washroom for leverage in moving from a wheelchair or walker to the toilet.

✓ A padded toilet seat ring that reduces the opening of the toilet to provide secure and soft seating for a child who is very slender or who needs longer potty sits.

✓ Toilet supports with chest straps, safety belts, padded cushions, armrests, and footrests.

✓ Safety rails and handlebars for support and a swing-away bar to mount by the toilet.

✓ Child commode chair, with adjustable height legs, swing away safety bars and commode pail. It also includes padded headrest, adjustable footrest, and seat belt.

✓ For children with difficulty in muscle control, check with your physician as to when is the best time to start training. Talk to him about the body signals your child needs to recognise to go to the potty. This may vary depending on the disability, so an individualised approach is required. A child with a disability may have a muted sense of body in general, so being messy may not be as bothersome to him as it is to others.

For children with special emotional needs, such as those with autism, the challenge can be mental in nature. However, they can associate happy feelings with positive actions. When they see mommy or daddy smiling and clapping after doing what he did, he can sense that he did something right. These actions can be pulling down his own clothes or flushing after he has done his business. Reinforce positive feedback with every small success, because they are all important.

Chapter 10: Designing a Potty-Training Calendar

Designate 3 days in a row

Mark them on your calendar. Remember that the three days must not be sandwiched during big transitions, or events that demand a great deal of attention or work.

This means one of those 3-day peekends if you can't get any time off from work (Labor Day, Memorial Day, etc). During these three days, do not plan to go anywhere.

You want to give yourself a chance to be consistent with this because consistency is the key to succeeding with potty training.

Plan ahead for how usual chores can be done during those days. If your child is in daycare, arrange for a rescheduling.

Prepare a variety of activities you and your child can do together

You can be out in the yard at times as long as you can manage to run to the potty at all times. Otherwise, it's much better to be indoors during those three days. Inside the house, carry on most activities in an area with easy-to-clean flooring. Prepare an assortment of books, crayons, markers, play dough, puzzles, blocks, and helpful television shows. You want to keep your child busy and happy during this 3-day process, and three days with a toddler inside the house takes a lot of creativity.

Have laundry done before starting

Ensure clean sheets and extra pajamas or loose trousers are available in case they have accidents once training starts.

Introduce high fiber foods to your child's diet

High-fiber foods help control constipation by keeping fluids in the stools, keeping them soft and easily passable.

✓ Offer a high-fiber, easy-to-eat cereal as part of your toddler's daily diet. Most toddlers will happily eat O's type of cereals that are high in fiber.

✓ Serve yogurts that have added fiber in them with meals. Toddlers usually love yogurt. Yogurts with added fiber are just as tasty and creamy as regular yogurt.

✓ Make sandwiches with high-fiber wheat bread. Try serving your toddler peanut butter and jelly made on high-fiber wheat bread or whole grain white bread. While whole grain white bread offers less fiber than 100 percent wheat bread, it definitely provides more fiber than traditional white bread.

✓ Make high-fiber vegetables like broccoli, sweet potatoes, spinach and cabbage an appealing part of your toddler's diet. You can serve sweet potatoes with a little butter and brown sugar, or add small amounts of spinach and shredded cabbage to a turkey sandwich. Vegetables like beans, sweet potatoes, peas, tomatoes and corn are all higher in fiber. Cook a sweet potato in the microwave for 5-7 minutes. Peel, then slice into cookie shaped circles and serve. Serve steamed green beans or cauliflower with ranch dressing for dipping. Frozen peas right out of the freezer are a nice, cool treat on a summer day.

✓ Offer high-fiber fruits such as apples, pears, and prunes to your toddler daily. Fruits are a painless way to add fiber to your toddler's diet. Feed fruits with a peel, since the peel has a higher fiber content. Prunes and apricots have a pro-laxative effect, in addition to being rich in fiber. Slice grapes or cherry tomatoes in half and serve with whole grain crackers.

o Core an apple, then spread a thin layer of peanut butter onto round slices. Avocados are very high in fiber, and a soft, tasty treat for younger toddlers. For variety you may want to serve a variety of small slices of fruit on a colorful plate or even in an ice cube tray.

✓ Serve your toddler whole grain pasta and brown rice, instead of their highly refined white counterparts.

Nutritionists recommend reducing cheese and other dairy products during the potty training period, since they can have a constipating effect. Instead, offer plenty of water, which will ease any constipation and fill that bladder up, giving plenty of opportunity to practice!

A fiber-rich diet will make potty training easier for you and your toddler, but it's also a great way to introduce healthy foods and build a foundation of good nutrition for life at a very early age.

Chapter 11: 3-Day Potty Training Method

Principles that make the 3-Day Method effective

Every child is different. Even among siblings, each will show readiness signs, respond to training, achieve mastery in his or her own unique way, which then makes for wonderful storytelling. But just because things don't seem to be working at the beginning in the way we expect, it doesn't mean "the method doesn't work" and toss out the method. That's why it helps to read this book several times BEFORE applying the 3-day method, and not while in the middle of it. After letting it simmer in your mind for several weeks while observing your child's responses and temperament, by the time you actually begin the 3- day training, you kind of know it "by heart" and not just "by the book."

You will by then have some idea how to innovate within the guiding principles of the 3-day method. You will be able to determine where to apply variation and where to be firm and unchanging. For example, you may innovate about what kind of rewards to give, and how, but you have to be firm about using real underwear (and not pull-ups) after throwing out diapers.

At the very foundation of what's fixed and what's varied, are principles that make the 3-day method of potty training effective. These apply to each child, regardless of temperament. Be prepared never to run out of:

Persistence

Potty training is a time when a child learns to make several connections between his own body sensations and functions and the use of brand new equipment. It takes time. So even if our child seems to gravitate between success and regression, or may suddenly seem disinterested, or may even seem to already get it, these are the times when we don't give up. There's a process going on and your child's mind and muscles are taking it all in, one at a time. We need to keep up success on our side of the training area, and eventually it will click. And it will be great.

Consistency

Sometimes we might be tempted to take shortcuts with the intent of reaching the goal faster. When that happens, stop. Take a deep breath. Resume with the same energy, responding to each pee and poo with the same actions. Consistency means being able to do it the same way all the time, without any action being loaded with any recrimination or frustration.

The pending process and potty schedule should not be interrupted. Don't even think of going back to diapers or pull-ups once your child has begun wearing underwear, even if he cries and asks for it or refuses to poop unless you put a diaper on him. If you give in, this will only confuse your child and weaken his body's resolve.

Consistency in the 3-day potty training method applies to all, whether with boys or girls, older children, children with autism, Asperger's, Down's, OCD, or any diagnosed disorder. It's about the parent being on top of the situation, working with the responses of the child. Most girls train faster than boys. But sometimes there are boys who get it quicker. Whatever the pace, as parents, we need to implement actions in the same way. Using this method, we don't sit back and say, "They'll just go when they are ready." There are

many things we have to introduce and help our child connect with. Otherwise, how are they going to know? Just like everything else, we teach them.

Patience

Whether it's learning to play the violin, whipping up a great souffle or making a blog video, everything takes patience to do well. Potty training in three days doesn't mean it is going to be easy, it just means it will take three days for a child's body to absorb the basics. There will be accidents to clean up depending on how much effort you put into observing your children, sticking to the potty schedule, and managing beverage consumption. Bed wetting and other issues may be encountered, and unless there is a medical reason behind such issues, which can be the case with bed wetting, being patient in your efforts gives you the results you are looking for. Focus with patience on what you are aiming for with your child.

Positivity

Everything about potty-training is good. Even the accidents have no negative side-effects. Things can only get better. It will work out in the end.

When you decide it's time to begin potty training, set your child up for success. Maintain a good sense of humor and a positive attitude — and encourage the whole family to be the same.

Love

Of course, love is why we're making the effort to help our child use the potty, but it can get tricky what is the most loving thing to do when he poops in another fresh change of new underwear. Often, it just helps to break down laughing and remember how round his eyes get when he knows he missed, or how great it is that he is even willing to try. For potty training, just like learning any new skill, we need to give our children and ourselves some breathing space and cut ourselves some slack so we can rebound with a smile every time.

No punishment, reprimands or negative behavior correction techniques

Accidents are going to happen so be prepared for them. Even children who have used the potty successfully for months occasionally have accidents. Don't make them feel bad for having an accident. Scolding will mean more months of potty training rather than fewer.

Remember this when you feel frustrated.

Instead, remind them to tell you when they need to potty so you can take them to the potty right away. Remember that positive reinforcement goes further, so always praise your child for a job well done or for trying.

There are several instances when a child who won't go in the potty will go the moment diapers are put back on. Don't be put off. No matter how tempting it is to revert to diapers or pull-ups, stick to underwear, even during nighttime training. It will be worth it in the end. The preparation period will help as you introduce your child to the potty a few weeks ahead of the three days.

If you are a disabled parent, by all means you can be actively involved with the teaching, playing, and non-physical aspects of potty-training.

Day 1

The first day may be the hardest, especially for working mothers who may not be used to staying at home. It's not easier for stay-at-home moms, but on a whole, the joys will far outweigh the pains for any parent who is prepared.

This takes a lot of patience and diligence. You will have to watch your child constantly for signs that they need to go to the potty. In the beginning, you may not pick up on their need to go until they are already going. As soon as you see them going, place them on the potty where they can and will finish going. As they go, talk to them about the feeling of needing to go. Say, "Did you feel that you were about to pee? When you feel like that, it means it's time to get on the potty." Be calm and reassuring. If they go in the potty at all, even just a little, give them a reward.

The potty should already be in the bathroom

It is better in the long run for the potty chair to be in the bathroom, than in any other location such as the garden or in front of the TV, so your child will learn to associate the potty with needing to pee or poo. Make sure your child's feet rest firmly on a floor mat or a stool while he is sitting on the potty. Help your child understand how to talk about the bathroom using simple, correct terms you decide on beforehand.

You and your child should eat breakfast

Lots of high-fiber food, cereal, fruit, and healthy liquids, juice more than milk.

Set the training tone for the day

When you take off your child's diaper upon waking, talk to them while cleaning them up. Tell them a bit of a story about how that is the last diaper they will be wearing.

Dress your child in clothes that are easy to take off – for example, loose trousers with elastic waistbands, rather than full body jumpsuits. In warmer weather, you might like to dress them in t-shirt and underwear, as you need to catch the moment when accidents occur. Many parents resort to the bare-bottoms approach, but again, it is better for the child to get used to wearing underwear AND feeling the need to go. While putting on fresh underwear, explain to your child "You're a big boy/big girl now…"

Make an event of throwing out the diapers

Let the child throw away every unused diaper in the house. Celebrate this transition. You may even call your parents or close friends and let your child spread the news. Once your child is wearing regular underwear, avoid overalls, belts, leotards or other clothing that could hinder quick undressing.

This is a big move for your child. If you celebrate it, the transition will be easier. Talk about how grown-up she is and how proud of her you are.

You may even treat it as a "Big Kid Potty Party" attaching balloons to the trash can as your child tosses out his old diapers. Then introduce the 'big kid' underwear (which he or she picked out beforehand) as a gift.

When you throw out the diapers, really take it out to the trashbin. Don't keep a few extras in storage.

Don't go back to nappies/diapers/training pants at all during the training process

Trading diapers for real underwear is more than just a change of outfit for your son or daughter. The diaper is the ONE thing that has remained a constant in their life so far.

Children wearing cloth diapers will feel more discomfort earlier than those clad in disposables.

But for those who have been used to disposables, leaving the comfort of super-absorbent layers is as if they are going through their "last stand." Siblings may grow up, favorite childhood items like pillows, blankets, and toys may change, and favorite food tastes alter from infancy. It will probably be hardest to give up a diaper. But once you take the diaper off, don't hesitate about it, or even think of reverting back when the going gets tough.

You may be training a second child and may find the potty-training period to be either a rerun of your eldest or a totally different scene. You may either use some or all of the pieces of new underwear you prepared at the start of the day. This is normal during the whole 1st day of training so you will be able to observe certain patterns from your child to help you adjust for the following day.

If they cry, gently explain they are big boy/big girl now

Weaning your toddler out of diapers depends on whether a consistent approach is taken. So if after the 3 days of potty-training, if she's at daycare or with a minder, nanny, or relatives, everyone needs to know what approach you use, so they can do the same, and prevent your toddler from becoming confused.

The more time your child spends out of diapers, the faster she'll learn. Children are more likely to understand how to use the potty if they're no longer wearing an absorbent receptacle, as the diaper is really a portable toilet.

Fifteen minutes after throwing out the diapers, go to bathroom, explain to your child what the potty is for, and what his goal is

Review how it is used, and give them a practice run to start off the day. Make sure it's very clear that this is the only place where they should go to pee and poo! It helps to designate only one potty where they need to go to relieve themselves. Parents may feel it convenient to let boys especially, pee out in the garden, but they could associate this with peeing in any open space, whether in preschool or in the park, as has often happened with my nephews. So it would be good to designate the potty as the only place to run when they need to go.

Some child may dislike sitting on the potty at first. You don't need to force them, but the next time they start going, set them down on the potty again. Eventually they will begin to see the potty as a welcoming place.

Have the mop, bucket, cleaning liquid nearby, but not within range of your child

Because messes are definitely going to happen, and it's probably not going to be in the potty the first time, arm yourself with all the appropriate cleaning materials and get ready for battle. You might wish to spread a large tarpaulin mat in the play area, if your floors are carpeted or polished.

Ask child at regular intervals if underwear is dry

Give positive reinforcement and praise each time.

Most children have a bowel movement once a day, usually within an hour after eating.

Most children urinate within an hour after having a large drink.

Instruct child, "Let mommy know when you have to go pee or poo, ok?"

Repetition is necessary as children have short attention spans. Only gentle reminders, it's best if your child doesn't feel pressured. If you're sure your child hasn't done a poo or pee in a while, ask him again, especially while he is doing something – he might get so caught up in what he's doing that he doesn't realise he needs to go until it's too late. This question entrusts him with a bit of responsibility. With older children, it's not necessary to keep reminding as the child can only turn it into a defiance issue.

DO NOT ASK the child if they have to go pee or potty

This provokes a kind of auto-response and often they will just reply no to get rid of the question. Besides, this is not a guarantee, as many pee/poo in their underwear just seconds after responding 'no.'

DO NOT take the child to the potty at definite intervals when he does not show signs of needing to go

Take your child to the potty only when you perceive he is about to pee or poo.

Some put their child to sit on the potty within 15 to 30 minutes after meals to take advantage of the body's natural tendency (gastro-colic reflex) to have a bowel movement after eating. Others turn regular intervals into a game, even using a "potty watch." But the child may get bored with the regularity or fixate on a more interesting aspect of the potty, like playing with the baby wipes. This 3-day potty training method has proven it is much better for a child to associate his body's need to go with the actual act of going to the potty. There's less disappointment, even on the part of the child, when he finds he really doesn't need to go at these intervals.

Offer liquids throughout the day

Give your child lots of fibre to eat and water to drink in a regular way so she doesn't become constipated, a condition which will make potty training difficult. Your child's diet is the best way to handle this, rather than buying fibre supplements.

Never force your child to drink if they don't want to.

Add prunes to the mixture of fruits. The prunes keep him from getting blocked up and constipated, and prevents a child from holding his poop for days just to avoid using the potty.

Day 2

Continue to apply the same instructions consistently from Day 1, with the wisdom learned from observing your child's patterns and responses. On Day 2, you can go out to the garden for one hour in the afternoon after they pee in the potty.

Don't show frustration at accidents or when the child seems to not get it yet. There are times when the child (who was used to disposables) is testing you. They just want to see if they can get the diaper back, as it was much easier to go then. Don't give in, just stay positive and happy and they will soon realize you aren't giving in.

It may be Day 2, but don't push your child. Relax and let him learn at his own pace: he is closer to getting the hang of it than before. Encourage him with gentle reminders and stories. What your child wants most is to please you, and praising him will tell him what a good job he's doing.

Often you may feel like Day 2 is going to be like Day 1, but it is possible that your child will begin to get it and there will hardly be any accidents. There still might be partial misses, instead of outright messes. On Day 2, your child may learn to recognize the sensation she was first feeling when she needed to go potty, so she will want to make it in time.

At first, a child may even be awed by the knowledge that she already knows what to do, but might be a bit awkward and try to hide. However, if you pick up on this as a signal, and put her on the potty, then give her a favorite book to help her relax - she will poo with comfort. "Hey that's great! You are getting it now!" Once a child is able to release successfully, the rest can come easier. But still, we should be consistent and not let down on following the training routine.

If a child can become difficult, start screaming, or resist any incentives, continue to stay positive and try to ease the pressure.

Day 3

On Day 3, you can go out for an hour in the morning and an hour in the afternoon – only after a pee. This helps reinforce the fact that your child needs to pee before heading out, and gives you enough time to get to the potty before the next one.

Wear only a shirt, underwear, and loose-fitting trousers for your child before heading out. Don't use diapers or pull-ups, as they can send a signal to the brain that there is something there to 'catch' the poo or pee, leading to regressions.

There may be a surprise on Day 3, especially if you approached the 3-day method with no pressure from expectations. Instead of having the same routine as Day 1 and 2, your child may suddenly get it and be free of accidents the whole day!

If a child is still not getting it, don't lose heart. His brain, body and muscles are already adapting. Be positive and remind your child of the training bits that he is able to do. It also helps to continue your usual enjoyable activities in between potty breaks – books, games, ice cream cones, cookies you both bake, etc.

A child's resistance will soften once the potty proves to be a comforting place. He may make an effort to verbalize and will willingly sit on the potty. It is the effort that counts – and of course it is an added bonus if there is a sibling to cheer him on.

Of course Day 3 could also become a meltdown, and any progress made on Day 1 and 2 is erased. Don't give up and stay calm. This will help to reflect and bring fresh ideas to the table.

There will inevitably be progress and will feel really good when you are finally done with potty training!

Chapter 12: Prepping for the Big Game

If you are slow and methodical in your approach to potty training, expect to see an amazing degree of cooperation. Go into it without planning, and you can expect chaos. The biggest predictor of success in potty training is timing it right, so be sure to be constantly on the lookout for readiness indicators.

Crouch down, look your child in the eye, and talk about warming up for the Potty Mambo. Bounce around with him — maybe some "Rocky" moves. Get him loose, and watch for a sign that he thinks you're making sense, like a head-nod or a little look that says, "I get where you're going with this." Start by letting your potty-trainee watch you and other family members use the toilet, so that he can have a firsthand experience. In childcare settings, he'll see other kids using the potty, which will pique his interest. The peer pressure will also help to get your child mentally ready.

Start letting your little one practice clothed potty-sits, and invite him to observe how you dispose of diaper contents. Talk the potty patter.

For your mental prep work, brace your perfectionist streak for ups and downs. Take comfort in knowing that all kids are eventually toilet trained. Most toddlers who are ready to train do wonderfully well, as long as supporters provide a steady stream of praise for their efforts.

Letting him watch you use the toilet

A terrific setup for potty training is letting your child watch you, your partner, and siblings use the toilet. If possible, have your child focus on same-sex folks (girls mimic grandmas, moms, and sisters, boys mimic grandpas, dads, and brothers). That way, he gets to see how people use the bathroom, and why they do what they do.

Praise is key. Instead of recycling tired sayings — "you do it because I said so" and "you'll do what I say while you're under my roof" — take the enlightened approach of "expect good behavior and you'll get good behavior."

The child has lots of things to process and make some sense of: the sitting down, the feeling of needing to go, the actual act of urinating, or having a bowel movement. For some children, making the connection comes quickly, while others are slower at the one-two-three. If your child takes longer to connect the dots, don't be concerned. Potty training is more a function of general temperament than intelligence. Remember, history shows that a number of geniuses were especially noteworthy for their full-tilt spaciness, which suggests that they probably weren't quick at toilet training either. No doubt, they spent half their time on the potty, pondering quantum physics or composing haikus.

Explaining the steps

Go snail-slow when you give verbal instructions. You have to allow time for your child to take in the information. Your child may be tomorrow's mega-genius,

but he still needs his potty steps outlined clearly. Carefully explain each step, from sitting down to flushing.

Getting clothes off and climbing on the potty

"Watch how I pull down my pants, and let's see you try it, too."

That should get him rolling.

"Now, let's see you climb onto the potty, just for fun."

He's moving in that direction; he's trying; he's on it! Of course, his pants probably are bunched up under his behind, meaning they could get wet. But he's feeling like a self-starter, and that's a good thing.

Doing potty business

Tell him that when you or his sister sit on the potty, both of you expect some poop or pee to come out. "And when you start using the potty, that's where your poop or pee goes when you do your business."

Talk about how nice it is that babies can potty in their diapers. And then, enthuse about how toddlers move on up to using training pants so they can get used to using the potty.

Wiping

Next, demonstrate how to tear off some toilet paper and wipe clean. "Try to get just a small amount because too much clogs up the toilet. Not too much, not too little, but just enough." Exactly like Goldilocks and the Three Bears. Talk about proper wiping, but don't overload him with information at this point.

Flushing

You can place some hefty wagers that your child is going to be pretty foggy as to why the toilet has become significant overnight.

And what happens if your toddler finds toilet flushing as his new best hobby? That's a normal response to a fun skill, but waste no time in pointing out toilets aren't toys; they are types of bathroom equipment meant to be used correctly.

Washing up

Show how to wash up thoroughly afterward. Again, be methodical in your explanation. Using soap and warm water, show your child how he can gauge whether he is washing long enough: "You have to sing the 'Happy Birthday' song all the way through." When he's only two, you'll be the one singing the song, but later, he will be able to do this.

Helping with the whole process

So, the more you handhold and illustrate how easy it is to use the toilet, the easier it will be for your toddler to adapt to this new equipment and his fledgling skill.

Encourage your child to get involved; let him help you flush and wash up with you.

Make the process as game-like as possible. Maintain a lighthearted attitude. If he's clumsy at it, giggle together.

Forget about lengthy explanations – your child has a short attention span and he will get bored easily.

Tell him he won't fall in if that concerns him. Some kids will inquire about the hole in the bottom of the toilet. If your child does ask that

question, tell him that it's large enough for poop and toilet paper, but not large enough for him to fall into. Explain that because the hole is small, he must not put too much paper in it or it will get stuffed up.

Chapter 13: Dos and Don'ts

Never nag your child into using the toilet

Instead, offer lots of praise and encouragement when he expresses interest and shows success. Explain to your child what a potty is and its purpose in terms that he can understand. You may want to do this through the help of stories that your child likes.

Parents are the first role models of children, and usually most of the young ones identify with the parent of the same sex

In this regard, try to get Dad to show your little boy how to pee and poo, and Mom to show to your little girl how to do the same.

When potty training, it is important to dress your child in clothes that are easy to take off

Avoid having them wear bodysuits, tight-fitting clothes, or overalls. Make sure they are comfortable and that their clothes can be removed and worn without too much fuss.

Avoid starting when there is a big event looming on the horizon

This can be when you are expecting a new baby, starting him in day care, travelling for a long period of time, moving into a new house or starting a new job. These big life changes warrant their own focus and attention. Doing so can throw everyone's schedules out of whack and places added stress. This sets you back a couple of steps and can cancel any progress you've made.

Think of your child as his own person

Once you make him comfortable enough to be in control of the situation, then you can expect positive results stemming from his confidence.

Don't be too hard on yourself

Whether you are doing potty training for the first time or not, this situation is also training for you. Do not stress about getting it done in a certain period of time. Each child matures at different levels in many different ways.

In this age of social media, do not tell the whole world that you are starting to toilet train

You will be bombarded with a whole lot of "helpful advice." If you want to share, wait until the training is completed.

Do not forget to take the potty with you when travel is unavoidable

As your child starts to warm up to his potty, avoid using public restrooms that may intimidate your child. Place your potty in a trunk or at the back of the car. Remember, familiarity is your friend.

If your child goes to a day care or kindergarten, inform the teachers that you are trying to potty train your child

Consistency is key, and the teachers can resume the training you have started at home.

Make your child happy and proud by using loads of encouragement and praise when he is successful.

Once your child starts using the potty on a regular basis, consider hiding unused diapers to avoid temptation

This may evoke memories for the child and make him regress. If he does ask for them, tell him that he is no longer a baby and that grown-up boys like him shouldn't be wearing them anymore.

Frequent changes help develop your child's discomfort with having wet diapers or pants. You will be helping with the "wetness complacency" once you change his clothes or diaper as soon as they are soiled. The feeling of discomfort lets him learn that it's not okay to be walking around with soiled or wet things clinging to his skin.

Never compare your child's training progress to his older siblings or any other kid

Pointing out that he didn't measure up to your desired level of success can demotivate him. Do not talk about potty-training screw-ups about other kids either. When the time comes for him to have a slip-up, he will not take it well. Honour his individuality instead and recognise how precious that gift is to him being his own person.

Chapter 14: Reinforcing Success

Do not expect a toddler to make the connection between sitting on a potty and using it. He can only recognise a pattern when he gets praise from you. Another very effective way is to set up a success chart where you can both track his progress.

Kids love stickers. Having a success chart where she can put stickers on can boost her motivation. Make a big deal about her getting stickers. Every time she is able to eliminate, you can give her a sticker. However, expect slip-ups to happen. Instead of a sticker, you can give her verbal praise. Reassure her that she may get the sticker on her next toilet successful trip. You are giving her something to look forward to, with her being motivated to succeed and get her badge of honour.

Giving out physical rewards or prizes also works, as does making good on a promise. You can tell your child that if she is able to poop in the toilet and flush it afterwards, you can both visit the park later in the afternoon. Toddlers and kids who are active would love this kind of reward, as it gives them the opportunity to do what they like best.

If your child rebels and asserts her stance to not use the potty or toilet, don't take this to heart too much. It can be frustrating, but exercise extended patience. Children are just testing you for backlash. Do not give in. Instead, smile and try saying the stuff below.

"You say you don't want to use the potty now, but we will see how you will feel about it once you get so good at it. You may even think it's cooler and better than using diapers. Later you can tell me how you feel about it, when you do use it compared to using diapers."

A younger child who is more resistant may need a special kind of incentive, one that is only reserved after she goes for a toilet break.

Do not show any negative reactions to the smell, consistency, amount, or appearance of her stool or pee. This way, she will not be able to associate bowel movements as something to be ashamed of, but rather as part of a normal body process.

Potty training is a time where you should be slathering on praises as often and as much as you can. Keep rewarding him for the milestones – his potty sitting effort, the way he removes his underpants, flushing the toilet, and for washing her hands right after. Clap your hands, give her a hug, and make her feel like she's a star. Tell him that eliminating his waste is the stuff that super cool kids do and that he can be just like his parents.

The next challenge is for you to keep the good habits ingrained during the whole process. Joining forces with other members of your family and other caregivers (teachers, day school watchers) will help cultivate in her a real-world approach to elimination. Gradually decrease the praises but keep them coming. Once your child has found his groove, reinforce it. The fanfare should calm down by this time but be consistent in letting her know that he's doing a great job and that you are proud of him. Make refresher comments every now and then and try to keep the momentum going. Let him know that help is there if he needs it. If you are not around, he can seek help from other adults and grown-ups like his grandparents, his teachers or his siblings.

An ideal outcome is one where the child feels a sense of pride in himself, and not fear. Make sure he isn't unsure of himself, as this will lead to regression when he is placed in a stressful situation.

Conclusion

You've listened to a lot of old wives' tales, read the magazines, and asked a lot of advice. You have gone out of your way to learn as much as you can about successful potty training. Remember that it is a challenging transition, but it can be fun if you choose to see it that way. Think of potty training as an opportunity for you to develop a strong bond with your child. Focusing on the good that comes out of it will motivate both of you and can also pave the way for the training to be a success.

You are the expert on your child. Never have an ounce of doubt or harbor feelings of inadequacy. You hold the magic keys to successful potty training. You can do it. Your kid can do it. Rock on with confidence and see you soon on the other side.

-- Freya Gates

Dear Reader,

Thanks for exploring this book with me. Now that you know how to potty train your kid from scratch…

…why not learn to develop his emotional intelligence and make some beautiful crochet projects as precious gifts for him?

You'll love the other books, because they complement this one.

Get them now.

Thanks,

Freya

P.S. Reviews are like giving a warm hug to your favorite author.

We love hugs.

https://www.amazon.com/dp/B07V2RBCX3

Check Out Other Books

Go here to check out other related books that might interest you:

https://www.amazon.com/dp/B07TBYHSF2

https://www.amazon.com/dp/B084ZYHQD4

https://www.amazon.com/dp/B084ZWWF3V

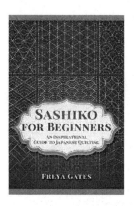

https://www.amazon.com/dp/B0868561GN

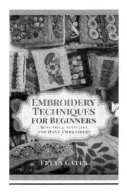

https://www.amazon.com/dp/B087X747QC

https://www.amazon.com/dp/B07FCWX28C

https://www.amazon.com/dp/B086D8PZT2

Bonus Free Material

If you would like a free book and keep up-to-date with the latest releases, please click on the link below to download:

Hand Puppets for Kids: A Guide to Toymaking and Improving the Motor Skills of Your Child

https://bookconnect.review/bookDownload.php?id=f2c4a5

Also, if you would like a list of free audiobooks, please be sure to Like our Facebook Page and send a message to claim them:

https://www.facebook.com/RylstonePublishing/

Made in the USA
San Bernardino, CA
09 June 2020